Confirmation

Student Journal

Compiled by
Michael Amodei

Benziger Publishing Company
Mission Hills, California

Special Editorial Consultant:
Irene H. Murphy

Design and Illustration: Mary Moye-Rowley

Nihil Obstat:
Sr. Angela M. Hallahan, C.H.F.

Imprimatur:
†Roger Cardinal Mahony
Archbishop of Los Angeles
February 7, 1989

The nihil obstat and imprimatur are official declarations that a book or pamphlet is free of doctrinal or moral error. No implication is contained therein that those who have granted the nihil obstat and imprimatur agree with the contents, opinions, or statements expressed.

Printed in the United States of America.

Send all inquiries to:
BENZIGER PUBLISHING COMPANY
15319 Chatsworth Street
Mission Hills, California 91345

ISBN 0-02-655942-0 (Student Journal)
ISBN 0-02-655943-9 (Teacher's Annotated Edition)

1 2 3 4 5 6 7 8 9 MAL 99 98 97 96 95

Contents

How to Use This Journal

Your preparation for the sacrament of Confirmation is a journey more than it is a class. You are learning with your heart and soul as well as with your mind. This Student Confirmation Journal is meant to help you stay in touch with yourself, with your family, with your sponsor, and with God as you prepare for Confirmation. Although this journal was designed to accompany the *Benziger* Confirmation Program, you can use it with any Confirmation book—or even on your own.

The word *journal* means "a book of days." People have always used journals or diaries to record their thoughts, feelings, impressions, and questions. This journal offers lots of space for your reflections. But it is more than just a blank notebook. This journal contains the thoughts and reflections of others who have traveled the journey of faith before you. It raises questions that ask you to think and to feel. And, in a special section, this journal offers some examples of Christian service projects in which you might want to become involved.

The eight sections of this journal all follow the same format. Each one helps you explore a gift of the Holy Spirit and a particular truth of our Catholic faith. Each section asks you to reflect and then to act on what you believe.

This is your book. No one will grade you on what you write. You do not have to share what you have written with anyone (unless you want to). Use different colored pens; doodle in the margins; paste clippings or favorite quotes on the blank pages.

May the Holy Spirit be with you on your journey of faith!

Created in God's Image

The Gift of Wisdom

"I believe in God, the Father almighty,
Creator of heaven and earth..."

I see
a light in you
that speaks of
a new creation.

Pope John XXIII

With God, I am a Co-Creator.
Here are my suggestions for an ideal world:

Ideal Weather:

Ideal Geography:

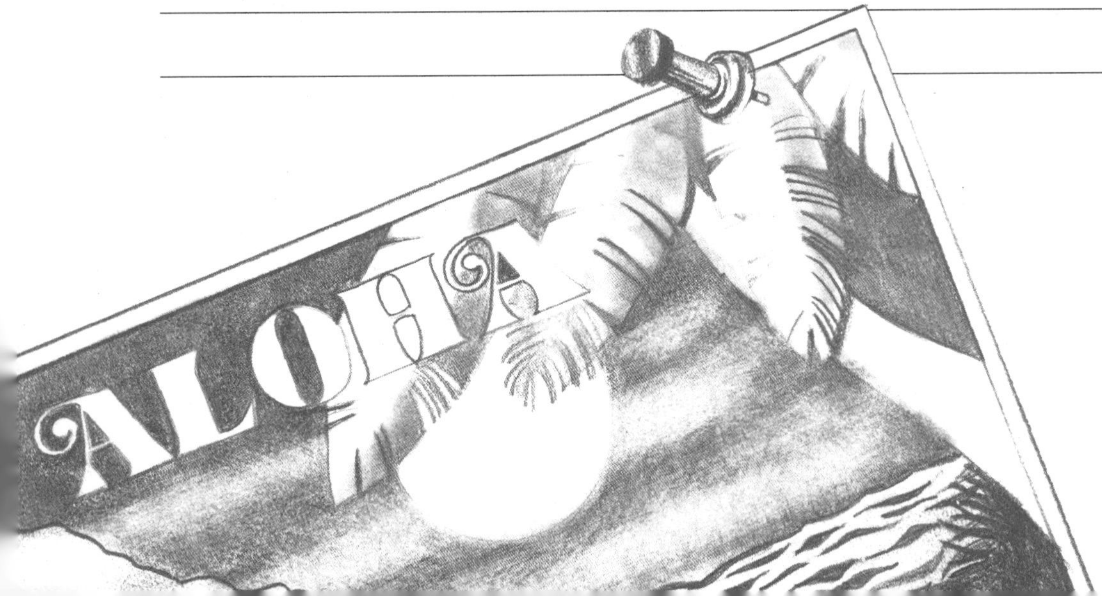

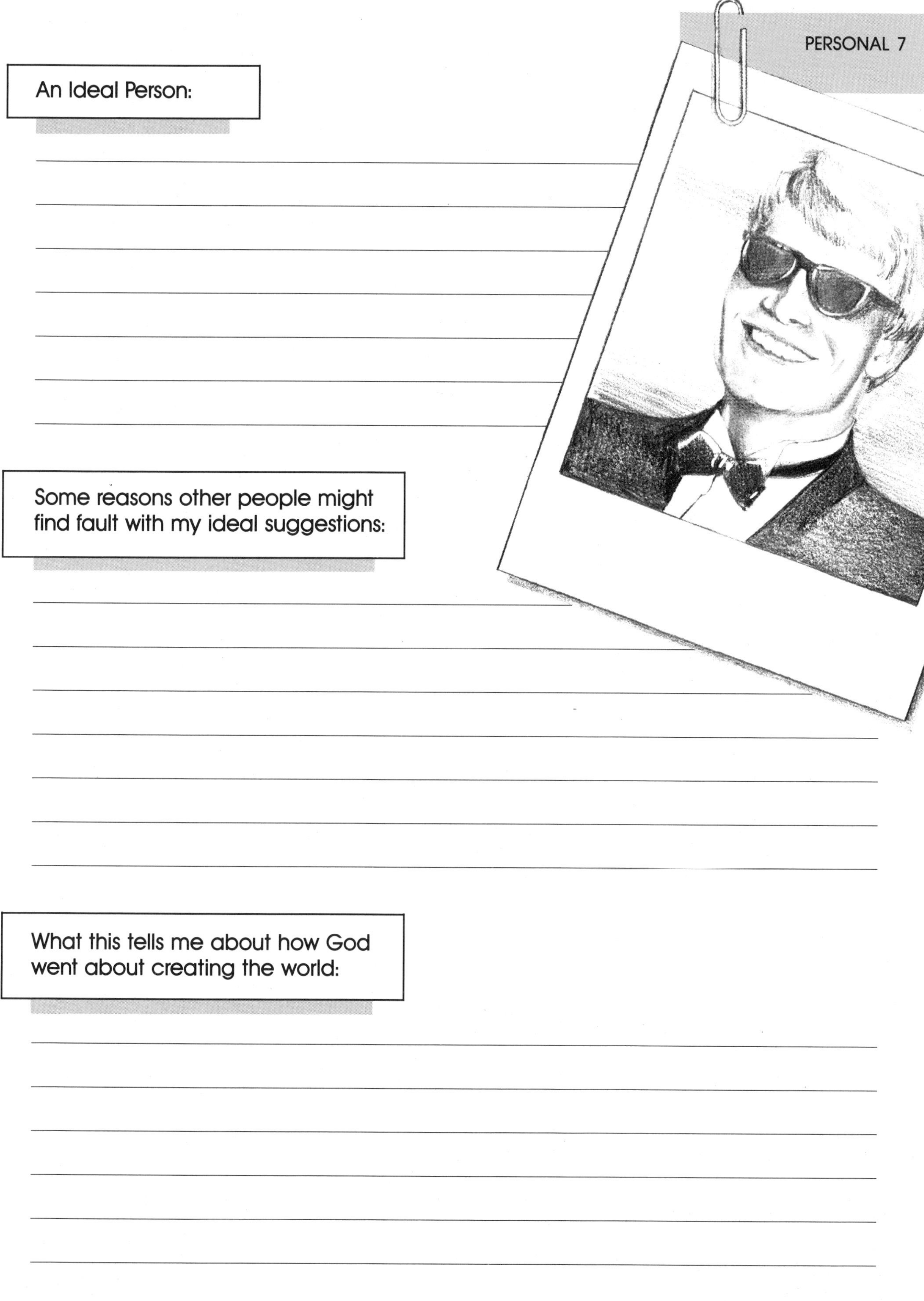

An Ideal Person:

Some reasons other people might find fault with my ideal suggestions:

What this tells me about how God went about creating the world:

My Life Is Important. Why?

Are you not more important than the birds of the sky?

Matthew 6:26

What did God do before Creation?
Was God lonely?
How did God always exist?

One God and Father of all, who is over all and through all and in all...
Ephesians 4:6

Before setting personal goals, why is it important to know more about the world's "big picture"?

Christian Service Project Reflection

Project Name: ______________________

Dates Completed: ______________________

What I Had Hoped to Accomplish
Best Experience/Worst Experience
A Neighbor I Loved
How God Was Present

______________________ ______________________
Parent's Signature *Sponsor's Signature*

2 The Jesus Story

The Gift of Knowledge

"I believe in Jesus Christ, His only Son, our Lord.
He was conceived by the power of the Holy Spirit,
and born of the Virgin Mary..."

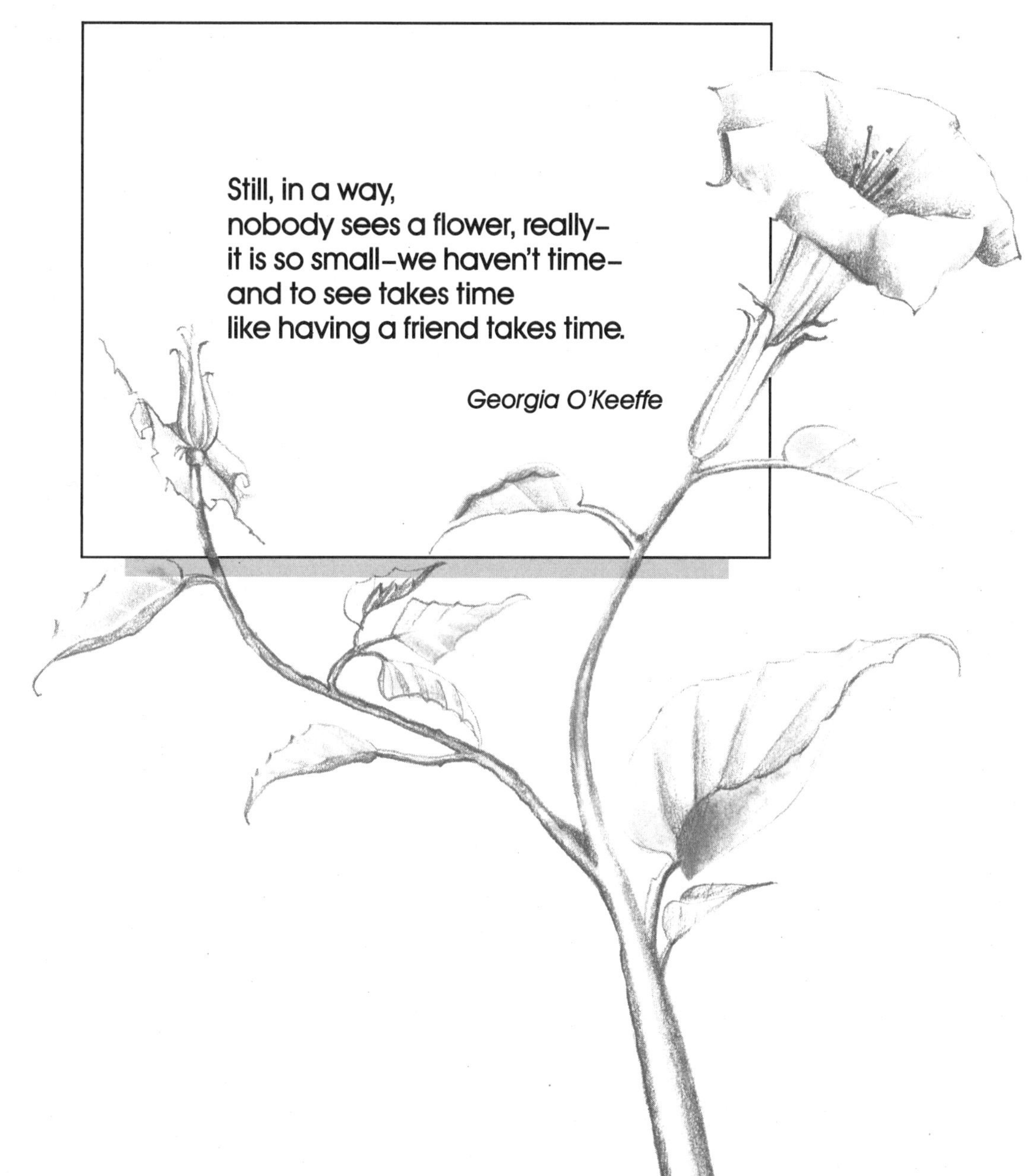

Still, in a way,
nobody sees a flower, really–
it is so small–we haven't time–
and to see takes time
like having a friend takes time.

Georgia O'Keeffe

I was God. I am God.

Yet, I never knew what it was really like to be human until a certain night in a stable, when I came into the world as the Baby Jesus. These are my first impressions of sight, sound, touch, taste, and smell. This is my first-person account of what it's like to be human. I've titled it:

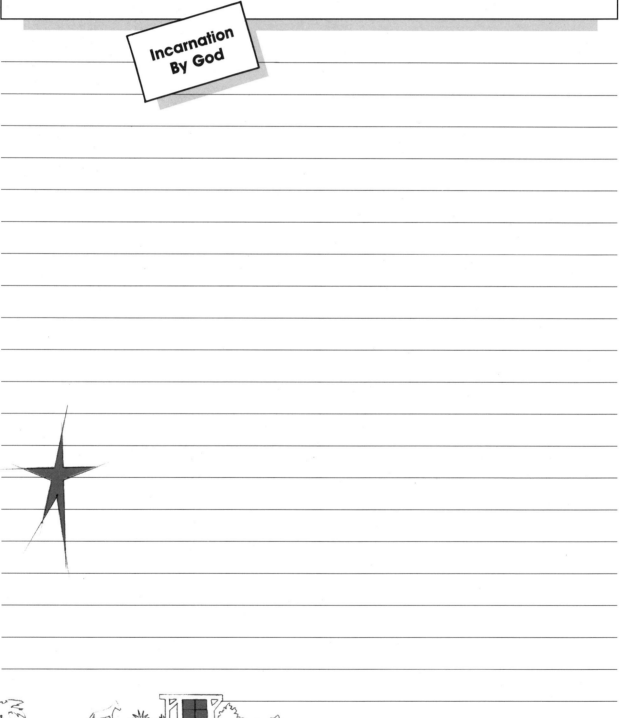

If Jesus were to be born into my world, my neighborhood, today, His story would read like this:

Why was Joseph afraid to take Mary into his home? Why are people afraid to take Mary and Jesus into their lives?

...do not be afraid to take Mary into your home.
Matthew 1:20

What is one interest, belief, or value that has always been a part of my life and will always *remain* a part of my life?

He is the image of the invisible God, the firstborn of all creation...
Colossians 1:15

Jesus is the Truth.
Jesus is love.
Jesus is "cool."

Really?
Write a letter to a friend telling why Jesus is the "coolest" of all.

Dear ______________________,

Your friend,

____

Christian Service Project Reflection

Project Name: ____________________
Dates Completed: ____________________

What I Had Hoped to Accomplish
Best Experience/Worst Experience
A Neighbor I Loved
How God Was Present

____

Parent's Signature

Sponsor's Signature

3 The Meaning of Eucharist

The Gift of Reverence

"He suffered under Pontius Pilate, was crucified, died, and was buried. He descended to the dead. On the third day He rose again. He ascended into heaven, and is seated at the right hand of the Father. He will come again to judge the living and the dead."

Worship, then,
is not part of the Christian life:
it *is* the Christian life.

Gerald Vann

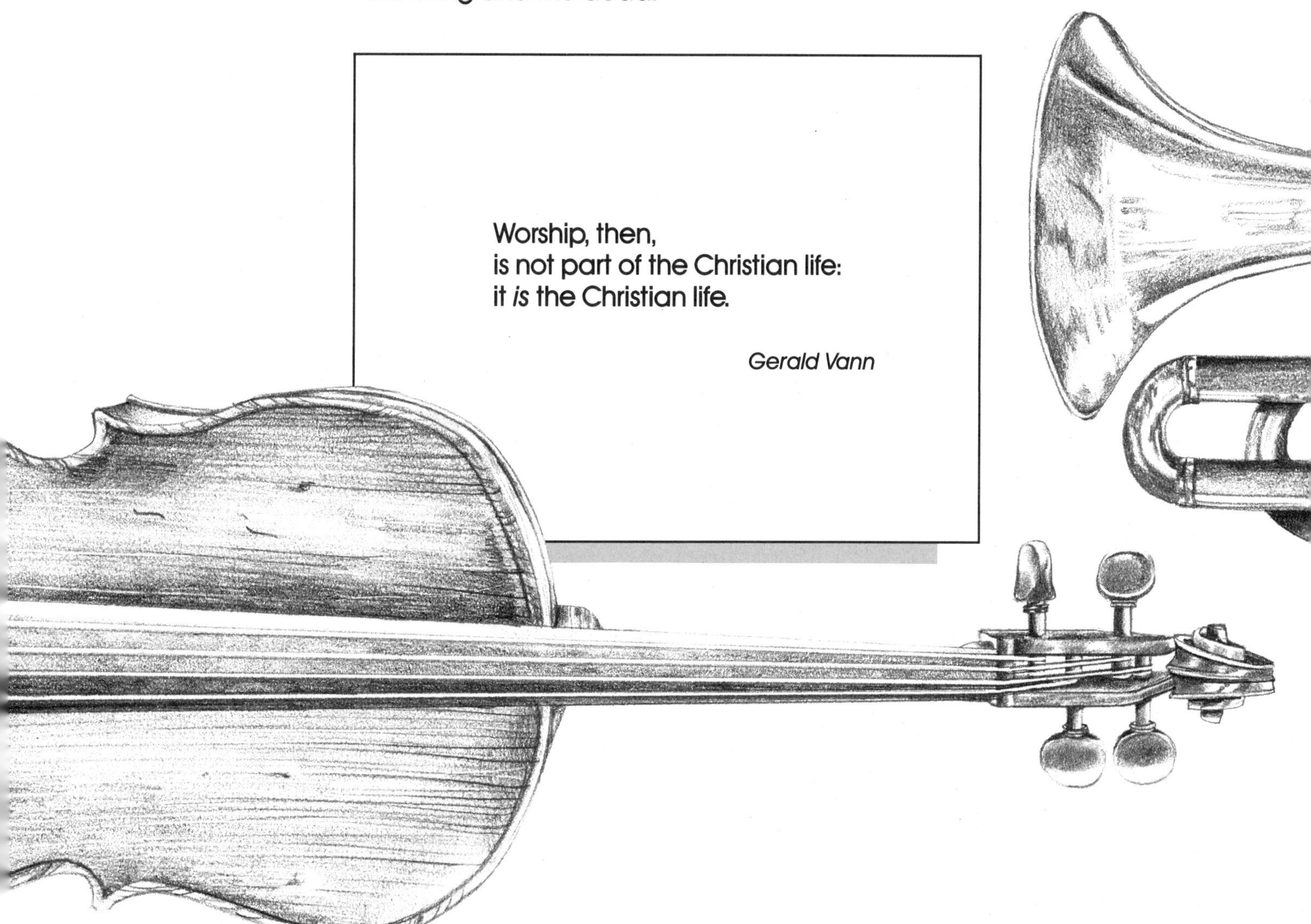

Meals I Will Always Remember

A wedding or holiday meal:

A meal when I felt like an unwanted guest:

A picnic or meal by a campfire:

An everyday meal with my family:

A meal with my closest friends:

What are some of your favorite places to pray? Why?

At what times in your life do you feel most like praying?

You have changed through the years. How has your way of praying changed?

He would withdraw to the desert places to pray...
Luke 5:16

My Own Prayer of Reverence

He was heard because of his reverence...

Hebrews 5:7

Tell how you experience God's presence at Mass when you:

Hear the Gospel

Hear the Eucharistic Prayer

Exchange the kiss of peace

Sing or listen to music

Pray the Lord's Prayer

Receive Communion

Christian Service Project Reflection

Project Name: ______________________________

Dates Completed: ______________________________

What I Had Hoped to Accomplish
Best Experience/Worst Experience
A Neighbor I Loved
How God Was Present

____

______________________________ *Parent's Signature*

______________________________ *Sponsor's Signature*

4 To Love and Serve

The Gift of Courage

"I believe in the Holy Spirit..."

Christ has no body on earth
but yours, no hands but yours,
no feet but yours...
Yours are the feet with which
He goes about doing good,
and yours are the hands
with which He is to bless us now.

Saint Teresa of Avila

I used to be afraid.
Then, one day, I wasn't afraid anymore.
I was given courage.

My Story of Courage

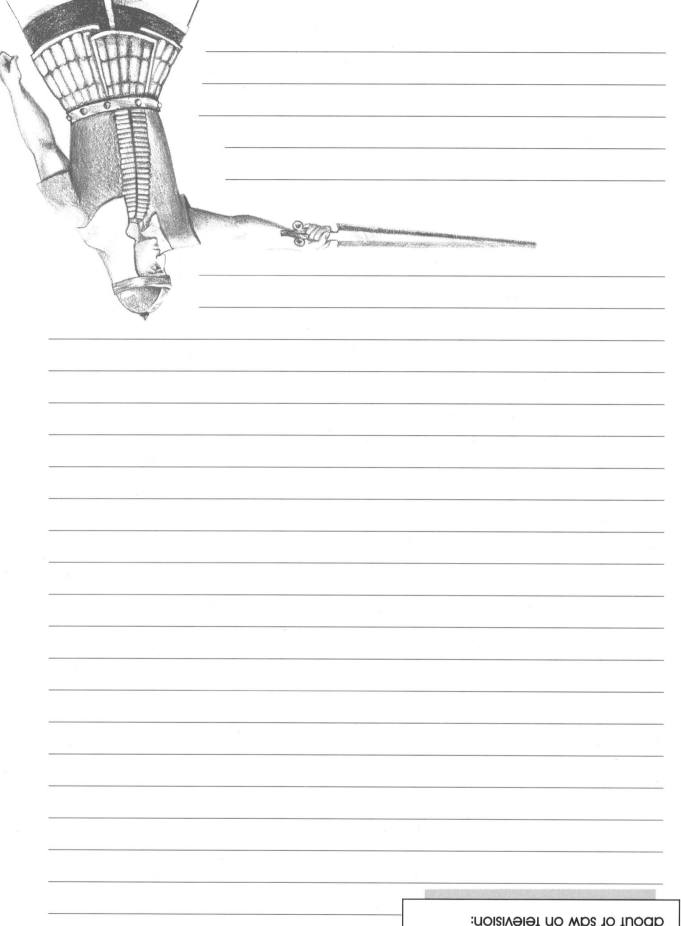

Here is a story of courage I read about or saw on television:

"Jesus washing His disciples' feet is like the principal climbing on the school roof to get a lost ball."

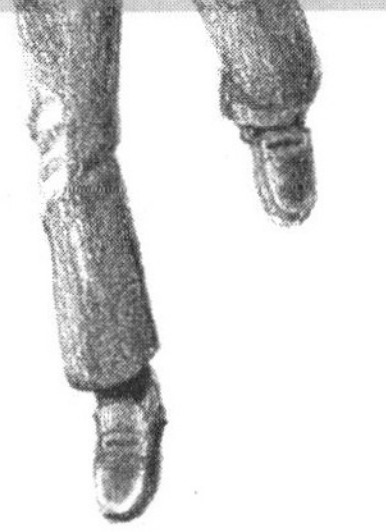

"Jesus washing His disciples' feet is like my spending my whole lunch period helping a third grader learn arithmetic!"

Make up your own analogies, comparing Jesus' humble act of service with surprising signs of caring that you see in your own life.

What I am doing, you do not understand now, but you will understand later.
John 13:7

When was a time when you were surprised by how well you spoke before a large crowd? What was the occasion? What did you say?

And they were all filled with the Holy Spirit, and began to speak in different tongues, as the Spirit enabled them to proclaim. *Acts 2:4*

Write the true story of how the Spirit has helped you to share the Good News of Jesus with someone else. Use the letters S-P-I-R-I-T to start the sentences or paragraphs.

S

P

I

R

I

T

Christian Service Project Reflection

Project Name: ____________________

Dates Completed: ____________________

What I Had Hoped to Accomplish
Best Experience/Worst Experience
A Neighbor I Loved
How God Was Present

____________________ Parent's Signature

____________________ Sponsor's Signature

5 Community of Believers

The Gift of Understanding

"I believe in the holy catholic Church,
the communion of saints..."

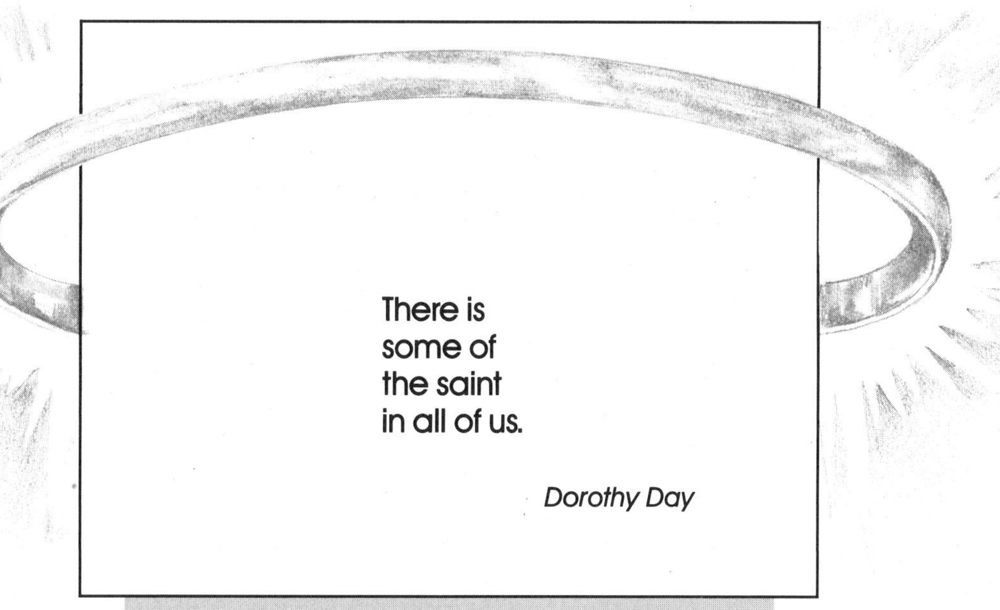

There is
some of
the saint
in all of us.

Dorothy Day

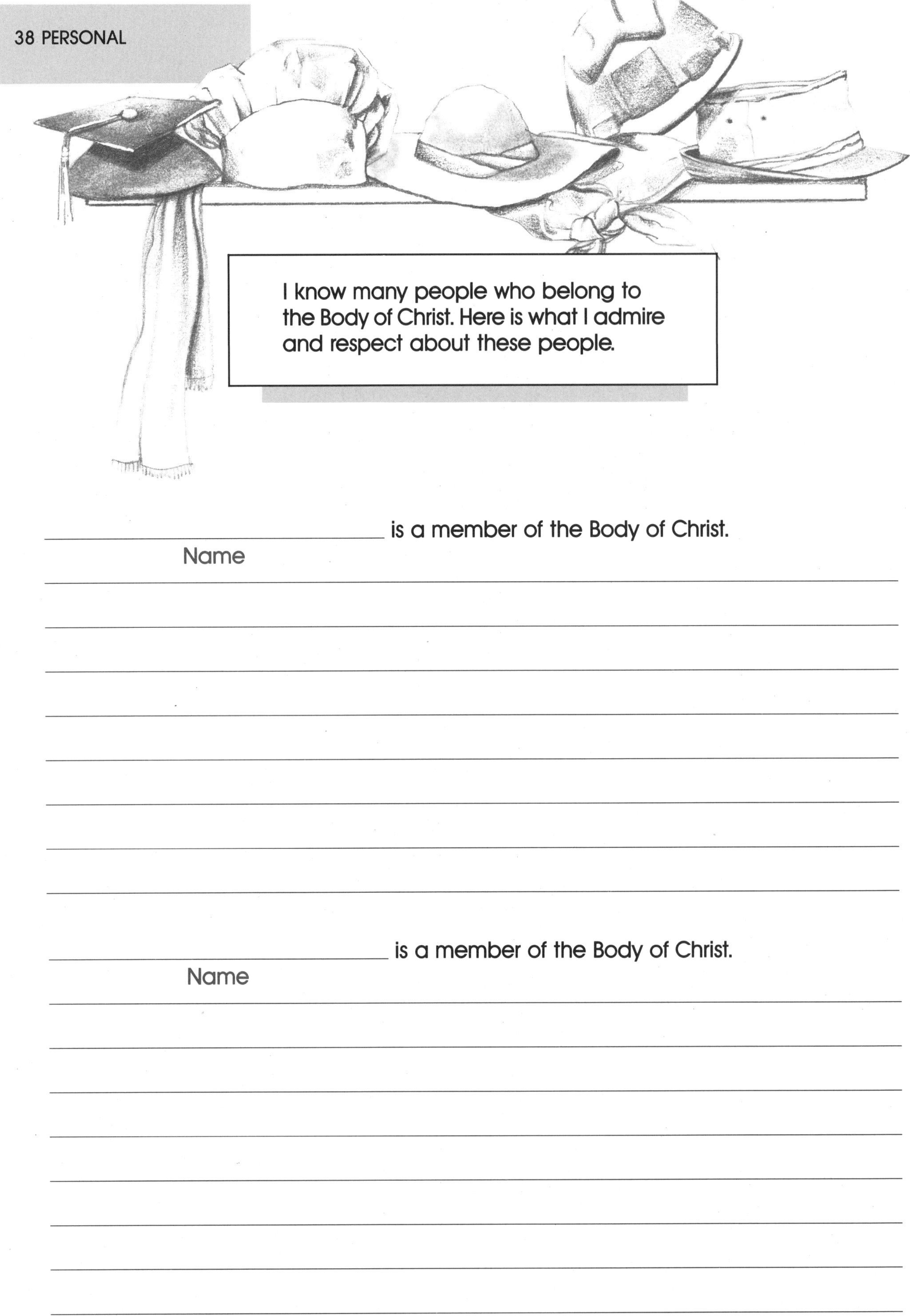

I know many people who belong to the Body of Christ. Here is what I admire and respect about these people.

____________________ is a member of the Body of Christ.
Name

____________________ is a member of the Body of Christ.
Name

________________ is a member of the Body of Christ.
Name

________________ is a member of the Body of Christ.
Name

________________ is a member of the Body of Christ.
Name

The Church is universal, with the pope as its head. Here is my letter to the Holy Father. It contains my questions. It also shares two things I want the Holy Father to understand about me.

Dear Holy Father,

Your child in faith,

____

All of you, be of one mind, sympathetic, loving toward one another...

1 Peter 3:8

When was a time when you shared another's suffering? When was a time when you shared another's joy?

If one part suffers, all the parts suffer with it; if one part is honored, all the parts share its joy. *1 Corinthians 12:26*

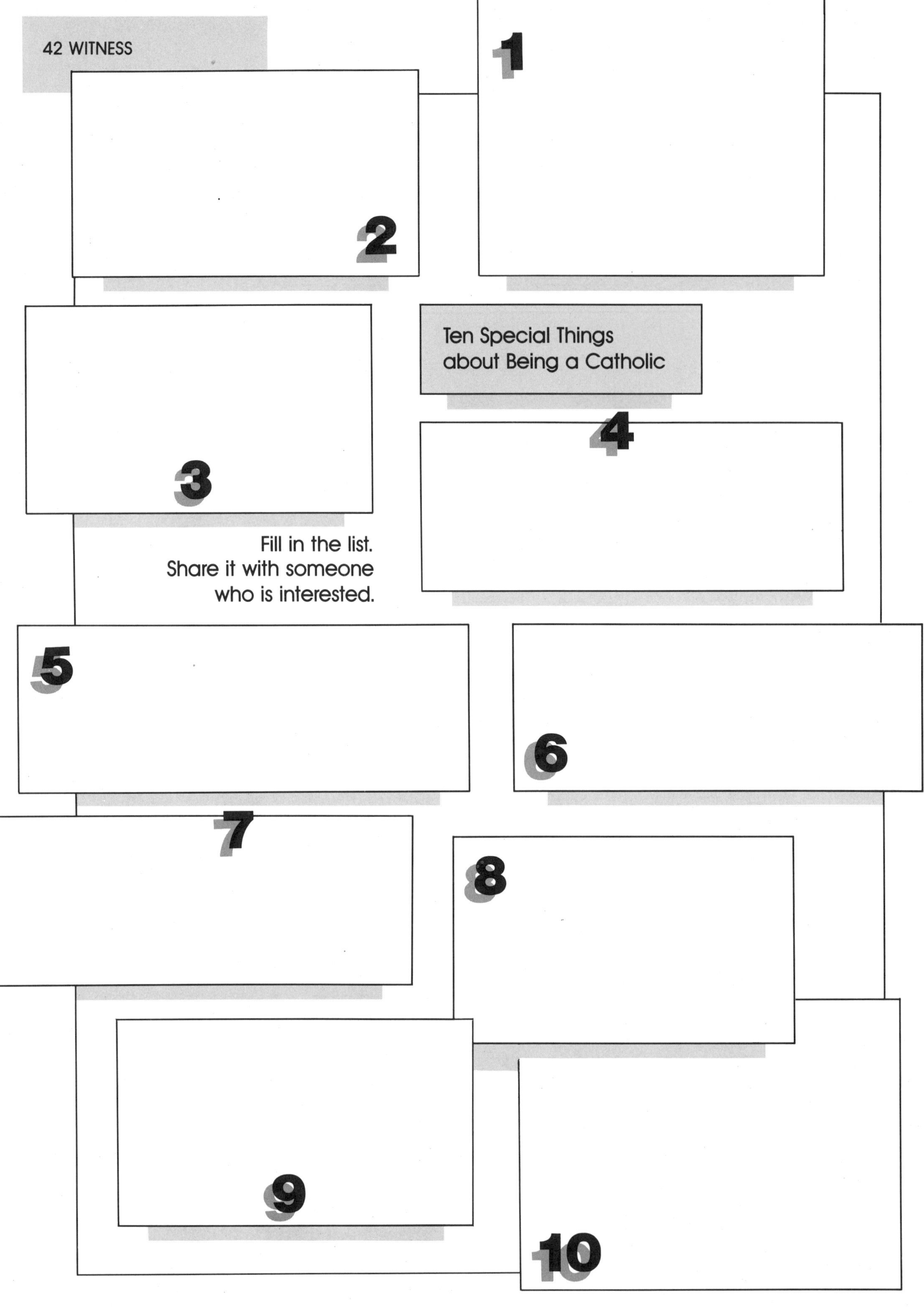

Ten Special Things about Being a Catholic

Fill in the list.
Share it with someone who is interested.

Christian Service Project Reflection

Project Name: ____________________
Dates Completed: ____________________

What I Had Hoped to Accomplish
Best Experience/Worst Experience
A Neighbor I Loved
How God Was Present

____________________ ____________________
Parent's Signature *Sponsor's Signature*

6 Covenant People

The Gift of Right Judgment

"I believe in the forgiveness of sins..."

The authentic Church
goes out to rescue people
from injustice
and brings them
the saving force of love.

Pope Adrian VI

Reconciled to God,
reconciled to my neighbor,
reconciled to myself:
that's what forgiveness means.

The Story of When I Forgave

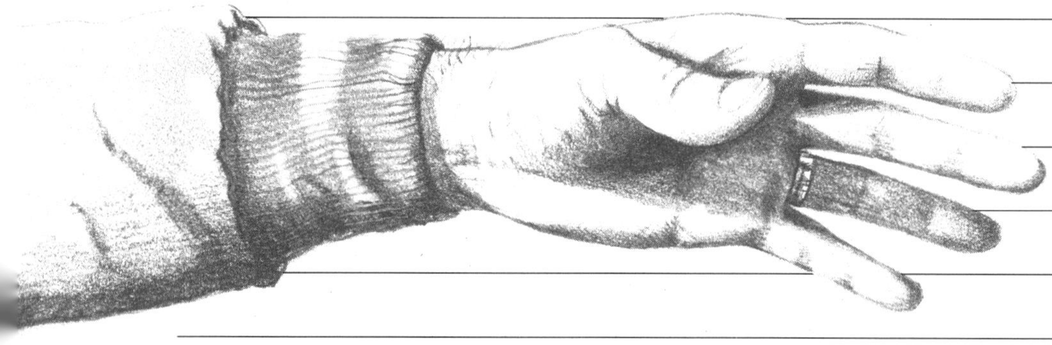

The Story of When I Was Forgiven

How could love help these hurtful situations?

A mother and daughter haven't spoken to one another in days.

Two girls are constantly picking on a new student.

A boy's best friend starts hanging around with a new crowd.

A boy lies to his teacher about completing a school project.

If I have all faith so as to move mountains, but do not have love, I am nothing.

1 Corinthians 13:2

These are the bad habits I would like to break:

This is the peer pressure I find difficult to face:

This is my prayer to the Holy Spirit for right judgment:

You will receive power when the Holy Spirit comes upon you, and you will be My witnesses... *Acts 1:8*

What would your life be like if you were not able to choose freely?
Who are the people in your world whose choices are limited?
What can you do to help them?

Christian Service Project Reflection

Project Name: ______________________________

Dates Completed: ______________________________

What I Had Hoped to Accomplish
Best Experience/Worst Experience
A Neighbor I Loved
How God Was Present

____

Parent's Signature

Sponsor's Signature

7 Journey of Faith

The Gift of Wonder and Awe

"I believe in the resurrection of the body,
and the life everlasting..."

Hallowed be Thy name, not mine.
Thy kingdom come, not mine.
Thy will be done, not mine.
Give us peace with Thee,
peace with others,
peace with ourselves,
and free us from fear.

Dag Hammarskjold

Answer one or more of the following questions:
What will heaven be like?
What questions would I like to ask God?
What does it mean to me to live forever?

Here is a collage–in words or pictures or both–of everything I think is "awesome."

Death is probably the most painful reality we humans face. Use this page to write what you feel about death, and about what the resurrection of Jesus means to you.

And if Christ has not been raised, then empty is our preaching, and empty, too, your faith. *1 Corinthians 15:14*

The Spirit's gift of wonder and awe helps us see signs of God's presence everywhere. Where do you see awesome and wonderful signs?

Awe came upon everyone, and many wonders and signs were done through the Apostles. *Acts 2:43*

What do you imagine your relationship with God and with the Church will be when you are the following ages:

With God		With the Church
	15	
	21	
	30	
	45	
	70	

Christian Service Project Reflection

Project Name: ______________________________
Dates Completed: ______________________________

What I Had Hoped to Accomplish
Best Experience/Worst Experience
A Neighbor I Loved
How God Was Present

____
Parent's Signature

____
Sponsor's Signature

8 Indwelling Spirit

The Fruit of the Spirit

"Amen!"

The gift of the Holy Spirit
closes the last gap between
the life of God and ours...
When we allow the love of God
to move in us, we can no longer
distinguish ours and His;
He becomes us, He lives us.
It is the first fruits of the Spirit,
the beginning of
our being made divine.

Austin Farrer

Come, Holy Spirit.
Come–when I am faced with temptation.
Come–lead me to Your service.
Come, Holy Spirit, and share my joy.

My Hopes for Life after Confirmation

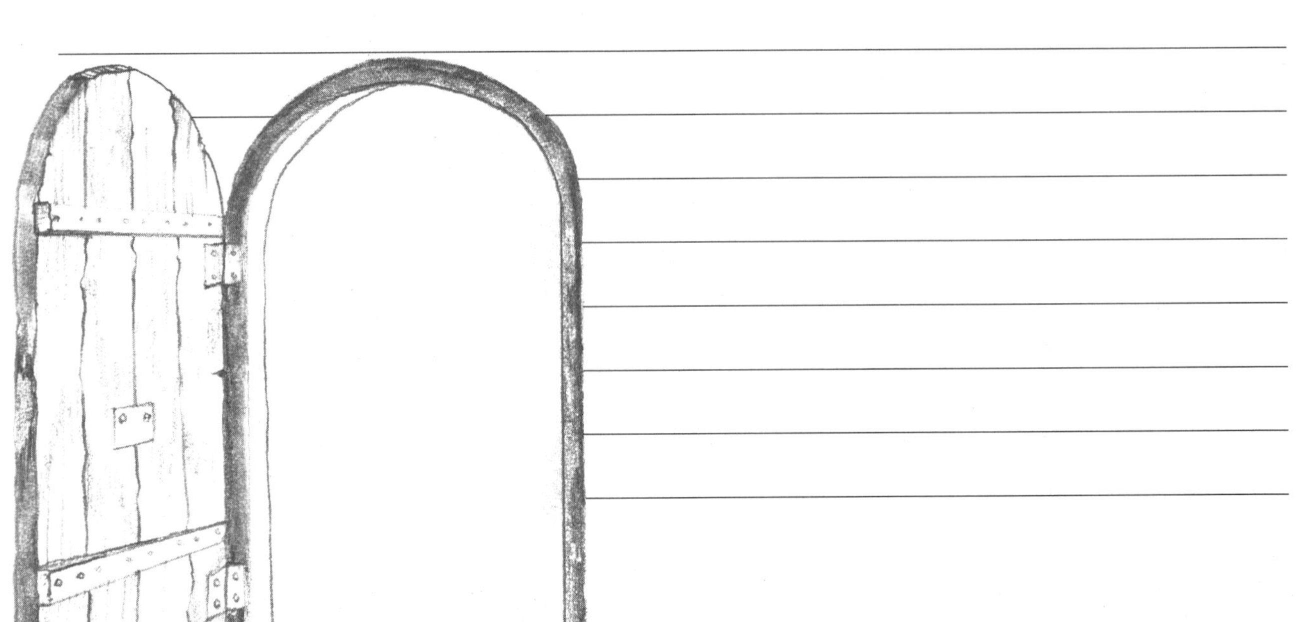

A Confirmation Prayer for My Classmates

Which fruit of the Spirit is most important? Which fruit of the Spirit have you been blessed with? Which fruit of the Spirit would you like to develop more fully?

If we live in the Spirit, let us also follow the Spirit.

Galatians 5:25

Use different colors and shapes and different styles of printing to make a collage of your spiritual gifts.

There are different kinds of spiritual gifts, but the same Spirit...
1 Corinthians 12:4

Choose one work of mercy "for the body." Choose one work of mercy "for the heart." Write how you will act to show these works of mercy.

For the Body	***For the Heart***
Feed the hungry.	Help the sinner.
Give drink to the thirsty.	Teach the ignorant.
Clothe the naked.	Counsel the doubtful.
Shelter the homeless.	Comfort the sorrowful.
Visit the sick.	Bear wrongs patiently.
Visit the imprisoned.	Forgive injuries.
Bury the dead.	Pray for the living and the dead.

Christian Service Project Reflection

Project Name: ____________________
Dates Completed: ____________________

What I Had Hoped to Accomplish
Best Experience/Worst Experience
A Neighbor I Loved
How God Was Present

____________________ *Parent's Signature*

____________________ *Sponsor's Signature*

Appendix

Christian Service Projects

> Whoever serves Me must follow Me,
> and where I am, there also will My servant be.
> The Father will honor whoever serves Me.
>
> *John 12:26*

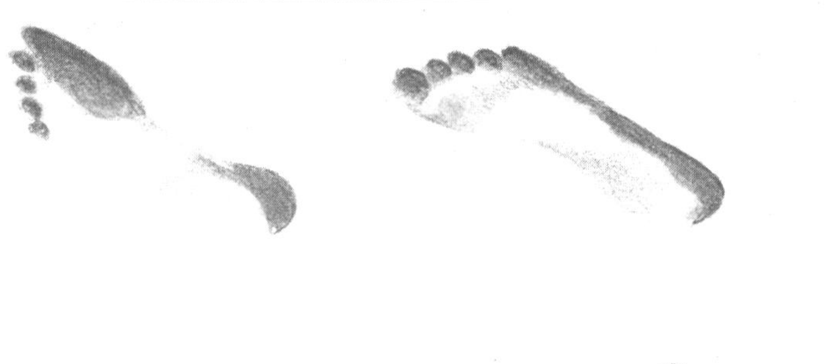

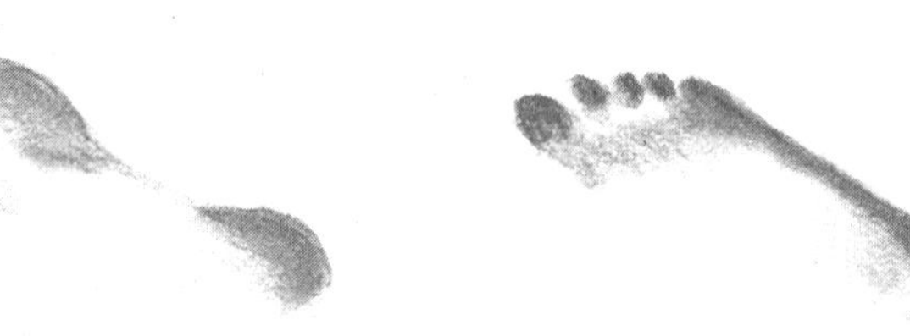

Two-Hour Vacation

Description

You provide free babysitting for the parents of younger children in your neighborhood for two hours on a weekday afternoon or two hours on a Saturday.

Resources/Materials

- Pen, paper for advertisement flyer
- Entertainment aids for the child or children you are babysitting:
  Nutritious snacks (approved in advance by parents)
  Storybooks
  A VCR movie suitable for children (check that parents have video player)
  Games, toys, puzzles, or sports equipment

Preparation

- Reproduce several flyers advertising "Two-Hour Vacations" for parents of younger children. Set up the flyer in the who, what, when, where, why format. Also explain on the flyer that you are offering this service as a part of your Confirmation program and that there is no cost. Distribute the flyers to families you know.
- Arrange times to babysit. Make sure, if the parents are leaving the premises, that you know where they are going and that you have a phone number where they may be reached and other appropriate emergency phone numbers.
- Meet the child who you will be babysitting. Spend some time with the child in the presence of his or her parents.
- Prepare two entertainment activities or ideas appropriate to the age-level of the child.

Procedure

1. Arrive at the scheduled time. Go over the emergency information with the parents. Wish the parents well on their two-hour vacation.
2. Explain to the child the two activities you have prepared. Ask the child which activity he or she would prefer.
3. Begin the activity. When you are finished, if there is time, allow the child to choose to do something else he or she would enjoy.
4. Make sure that all entertainment materials are put away, and food and dishes cleaned up, before the parents return.

Follow-up

Leave your phone number with the parents. Offer to babysit when needed.

Pray for Me

Description

You write letters to the vocation directors of three religious orders, asking for information on their particular orders and for prayers for the members of your Confirmation class.

Resources/Materials

- Addresses of religious orders and names of vocation directors
- Paper and pen
- Stamped envelopes

Preparation

Find out the names of several religious orders of priests, sisters, and brothers. Collect the addresses of the vocation directors of three orders. You may find this information in a local or national Catholic directory or in advertisements in Catholic periodicals. Your pastor or a sister serving in the parish may also be of help.

Procedure

1. Write three copies of your letter, one for each of the vocation directors you have chosen. In your letter, tell about yourself and your upcoming Confirmation. Ask for information on the particular religious order to be shared with your classmates. Finally, request the prayers of the men or women of the order for you and your classmates as you prepare for Confirmation.
2. Include a self-addressed, stamped envelope with each letter so that the vocation director can send information to you.
3. Mail your letters.

Follow-up

- Prepare a written or oral report, sharing the information you received from the religious orders with your classmates.
- Write a thank-you letter to the vocation directors on behalf of your classmates.
- If you wish, continue your correspondence with any members of the orders who responded to your requests.
- Include prayers for religious vocations in your daily prayer.

Garden of Life

Description

You will care for one or more house plants, seeing your work as a symbol of your spiritual growth as you prepare for your Confirmation.

Resources/Materials

- House plant with container and soil
- Watering pitcher
- House plant fertilizer (optional)
- Artificial lighting (optional)
- Notebook and pen

Preparation

Choose a plant suitable for indoors. This is usually based on how much light is needed for the plant to grow. Some common houseplants are fern, cactus, corn plant, ivy, and African violet. You may also choose to grow your own plant from a seed.

Procedure

1. Keep your house plant away from other plants for the first two or three weeks to make sure your plant is free from bugs or diseases. Also, keep your plant out of direct sunlight unless directed, and give it an extra bit of water during this period.
2. After the two-week period, water your plant only when it needs it. The general rule is that a plant should be watered only when the soil just under the surface feels dry. Water your plants in the morning, using lukewarm water.
3. Use a spray bottle or mister filled with water to wash your plant about once every two weeks. This removes the dust or bugs that may be on the plant's leaves.
4. If necessary, apply house plant fertilizer to the soil of your plant. Follow the directions on the fertilizer's package.
5. In your notebook, keep track of your plant's development. Be sure to note the name of the plant, where you got it, the kind of care given, and any changes or signs of growth that you notice.

Follow-up

- If your plant outgrows its container, repot it into a larger container. Use packaged potting soil and be careful not to damage the plant's roots.
- In your notebook, write a short story titled "Growth." Base your story on your own spiritual growth compared to the physical growth of your plant. Share this story and your plant with your classmates.
- If possible, present your plant as an offering during the Mass of Confirmation.

Good Person File

Description
You will keep a diary of newspaper and magazine articles that describe people who serve their neighbors.

Resources/Materials
- A looseleaf notebook with paper (8½" x 11")
- A two-week supply of the daily newspaper or several news magazines
- Scissors and glue
- Pen

Preparation
- Purchase the notebook and paper.
- Arrange with your parents to use the daily newspapers or news magazines *after* everyone in the family is finished with them.
- Develop the habit of looking for good or positive information in every story you hear, see, or read about.

Procedure
1. When you find a newspaper or magazine article that describes actions of service or caring, cut it out and attach it to one page of your notebook. Look for stories about people who help the poor, sick, elderly, or other people in need. You may also attach only a part of a story if it is the part that mentions the example of positive behavior.
2. On the same page or on the next page in your notebook, write some personal comments on the example of service you observed in the article. Your comments may fit one or more of these categories:

   A Prayer
   How the Holy Spirit Was Present
   What I Learned from this Example
   How the World Is Now a Better Place

   Or, you may write comments about the article in any other form that you wish. Place the date of the article below your comments.
3. Continue your survey of positive news articles for fourteen days. See how many articles you can collect. For extra credit, you may also describe in writing examples of service or caring that you see or hear in TV or radio news.

Follow-up
- Title your notebook.
- Share two or three of your favorite examples in a classroom presentation.

This Is Your Life

Description

You and your sponsor arrange, produce, and present a "This Is Your Life" skit for a mutual friend or relative.

Resources/Materials

- Paper and pen for writing the "This Is Your Life" skit
- Construction-paper folder to contain the final "This Is Your Life" script
- Friends, relatives, or acquaintances who can give testimonials or share memories of the subject's life as a part of the presentation
- Refreshments for a post-presentation reception

Preparation

- You and your sponsor make separate lists of friends or relatives who need cheering up and who might be good subjects of a "This Is Your Life" skit.
- Discuss your lists and choose a subject. Gather facts on the person's life. List the ways this person has served and loved others through his or her life. Ask other friends to participate in your presentation by giving personal testimonials about the subject. These incidents will be included in your script.
- Schedule a convenient time and place to meet with the person you have chosen and surprise him or her with the presentation. Make sure that you and your sponsor have enough time to write the skit and prepare the presentation. Don't give away the secret!

Procedure

1. You and your sponsor write the script. Include important factual information about the person's life, such as date and place of birth, education, employment, and marriage. The main text of your script, however, will be recountings of the good and sincere ways in which your subject has served others.
2. You and your sponsor meet the person at the scheduled time and place. Arrange for any additional guests to also be there. Think of a creative way to surprise your subject.
3. You and your sponsor share the narration in reading the script of "This Is Your Life."
4. After the presentation, host a reception for your subject and guests with the refreshments you have prepared. Let your subject keep the script as a memento of this special occasion!

Follow-up

After the reception is over, talk about the "whys and hows" of the presentation with your subject. Express your own feelings about what the person means to both of you.

"What's Happening" Journal

Description

You prepare a seven-day news diary for a person detained in a juvenile detention center. The diary highlights important news events from society in general, as well as personal entries offered by you. You share the journal with your sponsor before you and your sponsor arrange for it to be delivered to the juvenile detention center.

Resources/Materials

- A journal or notebook with writing lines
- Pen
- Current newspapers, magazines, or any other interesting periodicals

Preparation

- Meet with your sponsor to discuss the project and to call the visitor's coordinator of the local juvenile detention home. Your sponsor should explain the project to the coordinator, asking the proper procedure for either sending the project by mail or delivering it in person. The diary may be presented to one person or to a group of people living in the home.

Procedure

1. Complete the diary over a seven day period. You may wish to follow this daily format:
    - What's Happening in *The* World
      Include important news, sports, or entertainment events you find in the newspaper. You might wish to glue newspaper stories into the journal.
    - What's Happening in *Our* World
      Write about something that would specifically interest teenagers, such as popular music, recently-released movies, or news about celebrities.
    - What's Happening in *My* World
      Include personal things that interest you, like what you do for fun with your friends or what subjects you like in school. Also, you might explain your preparation for Confirmation.
2. Deliver the diary to the juvenile detention home with your sponsor.

Follow-up

Continue your correspondence with the people at the home. Write letters or arrange to visit the home on an open house day.

Prayer of the Poor in Spirit

Description

You and your sponsor will spend an hour together in church in personal prayer. In the Hebrew Scriptures, the poor in spirit were known as the *anawim*–those who placed their confidence in God alone. For the hour of prayer, you and your sponsor take the role of the anawim.

Resources/Materials

- Whatever scriptural or spiritual reading materials or devotional aids (the Rosary, the Stations of the Cross) you and your sponsor choose to assist you in prayer

Preparation

- Decide on a time when both you and your sponsor are able to spend one hour in prayer.
- Decide what form the hour of prayer will take. Here are some suggestions:
    1. Pray the Stations of the Cross.
    2. Recite three decades of the Rosary.
    3. Silently read Scripture passages based on the theme of "poor in spirit" (Isaiah 61:1–3; Psalm 90; Job 38, 39; Luke 12:22–34).
    4. Read together from spiritual books.
    5. Pray or meditate in silence.

Procedure

1. Pray together the Lord's Prayer. Reflect on your call to spend time with God as faithful and dependent servants.
2. Begin the main portion of your prayer, doing whatever both of you have decided on. In the case of a Rosary or Stations of the Cross, complete the devotion together. If you will do silent Scripture or spiritual readings, you may wish to move to separate areas of the church.
3. Sit with your sponsor during the final ten minutes. Quietly reflect on what it means to be dependent on God. Conclude by alternating petitions seeking God's aid for the world's *anawim.* Use this format: "For the (hungry) we pray: Lord, hear us."

Follow-up

During an informal meeting with your sponsor, talk about how you felt during the hour of prayer.

Patience Prayer Cards

Description
You make wallet-sized prayer cards to be used throughout the day.

Resources/Materials
- Blank 3″ x 5″ cards
- Pen and markers

Preparation
Think about times during the day when you must wait. Discuss these times with your sponsor. Examples of waiting: in traffic, movie lines, lunch lines, bank lines, grocery lines, and waiting for meals.

Procedure
1. Make cards for two times during a day when you must wait and two times during a day when your sponsor must wait. On the front of the card, list several positive things that you can think about and do while waiting. On the back of the card, write a brief Scripture passage with the theme of waiting, endurance, humility, or meekness. Scripture suggestions: Proverbs 16:19; Micah 6:8; 2 Corinthians 1:3–5; Luke 9:22; Job 42:1–6. Decorate the borders of each side of your cards.
2. Present your sponsor's cards to him or her.
3. Share a brief prayer together. You may wish to follow this format:
   - Opening Prayer (Compose your own prayer for patience, meekness, or endurance)
   - Scripture Reading (Choose Old or New Testament reading to fit your theme)
   - Petitions (Choose a response such as, "Lord, help us to be more patient")
   - Final Prayer (Pray a traditional prayer, such as the Lord's Prayer, together)

Follow-up
- Make prayer cards for family members or friends, using this or any other theme.
- Attend Mass with your sponsor. Arrive one-half hour early for private prayer.

Bike Ministry

Description

Students organize a collection and distribution service for magazines, newspapers, and other current periodicals. Groups of seven to ten students take orders and deliver the periodicals to elderly shut-ins who wouldn't otherwise be able to acquire them.

Resources/Materials

- Periodicals (collected from members of the group or from friends or neighbors)
- Bikes, skateboards, or another suitable form of transportation
- Backpacks for carrying periodicals
- Order forms (index cards will do)
- Master inventory list with pick-up and delivery schedule

Preparation

- Ask pastor or parish minister to list people who might be interested in such a service.
- Write introductory letters to the people, explaining the proposed service.
- Collect and continually update the periodicals.
- Plan pick-up and delivery schedule coordinated with your inventory of periodicals and the times that group members are able to complete the work.
- Use two order forms for each delivery. Note the materials borrowed, the delivery date, and the pick-up date. The second copy will be for your group's records.

Procedure

1. Mail the introductory letters to the people on your list. Make sure you list all the names of periodicals you have collected. Ask for suggestions for other periodical titles. Include a phone number where a member of your group can be reached. Your group may also wish to advertise in the parish bulletin.
2. Accept orders by phone and arrange delivery and pick-up times.
3. Assign one person to be in charge of the master inventory and delivery/pick-up order forms.
4. Form teams of two to carry out delivery, making sure you are courteous and helpful in explaining the service to your clients.

Follow-up

- Make preparations to pass on the program to another group of students. Inform the people who use the service that a new group will be participating.
- Occasionally visit the new people you have met.

Sunday Greeters

Description

Form a group of seven to ten students to serve as "greeters" for Sunday Mass. Members of your group stand near each entrance of the church, offering words of welcome to the parishioners. After Mass, your group sits together at a table outside of the church, answering questions about your Confirmation preparation.

Resources/Materials

- Table and chairs
- Poster paper, paint and tape
- Copies of your Confirmation or religion textbook, and examples of completed class projects

Preparation

- Explain the project to your pastor, and obtain his permission to carry it out at one or more of the Sunday Masses.
- Paint the words "Preparing for Confirmation" (or "Confirmation Catechumenate," if this term is used in your parish) on a table-sized piece of banner paper.
- Assign teams to each church entrance, reminding members to meet at their assigned places approximately 15 minutes before Mass begins.
- Set up the chairs and table with banner before Mass. Display textbooks and classwork on the table.

Procedure

1. Before Mass, station at least two people at each side or rear entrance of the church and at least four people at the main entrance. Stand in pairs on each side of the doorway.
2. Welcome parishioners with a smile and a simple greeting, such as "Good morning" or "How are you today?"
3. After Mass, all group members should sit at the discussion table. Politely answer parishioners' questions about your involvement in Confirmation preparation. Show samples of your work. You may ask parishioners to sign a guest book.
4. Make sure you return the table and chairs to the place where you borrowed them.

Follow-up

- If possible, send invitations to your Rite of Enrollment ceremony or Confirmation to the parishioners who signed your guest book.
- At a future meeting, allow group members to share their reactions to this experience.

School Intramurals

Description

Seven to ten students organize and oversee an afterschool intramural program for younger students.

Resources/Materials

- Paper for signups
- Permission sheets for parents to sign
- Sports equipment
- Play area

Preparation

- Decide on a team sport that both boys and girls can play. Suggestions include kickball, 4-person soccer, softball, or over-the-line. Be sure your group is familiar with the rules and procedures of the game you choose.
- Determine the day, time, and place of the program.
- Copy and distribute invitations with attached parent permission slips for students in Grades 1–3 or Grades 3–5.

Procedure

1. Choose captains from among your group to draft and organize teams from among students who turned in permission slips.
2. Print and distribute "league" schedules to all participants.
3. On game days, members of your group fulfill the following functions: captains, scorekeepers, referees, spectator supervisors, equipment managers, timers.
4. Group leader should remind both teams of their next games.
5. Along with an adult supervisor, help care for the students until they have been released either to their parents or to a school day-care program.

Follow-up

- Stage a championship game between the top two teams during the school day. Invite the appropriate classes to watch.
- Arrange for teams to have a party at the end of your group's participation. Provide snacks.
- Select award winners and present ribbons or certificates in these categories: Most Spirited, Most Improved, and Best Attendance.

Individual Tutoring

Description

Seven to ten junior-high students provide tutoring sessions in academic subjects to children in elementary grades.

Resources/Materials

- Writing materials
- Appropriate textbooks or workbooks
- Student Report Forms

Preparation

- Ask assistance and permission from teachers and parents in setting up the tutoring program.
- Pair one member of your group with each child that needs tutoring.
- Schedule your tutoring sessions individually, before or after school, in an appropriate place at school or at the child's home.
- Have the child's teacher prepare a list of materials you can use to help the child.

Procedure

1. Working individually with a child, use one or more of the following lesson suggestions:
    - Review basic math skills (addition, subtraction, multiplication, division).
    - Help the child practice printing the alphabet or developing handwriting skills.
    - Have the child read you a story.
    - Read the child a story. Ask him or her to tell you what the story was about or draw a picture to illustrate its meaning.
    - Help the child study spelling words or review historical or geographical facts.
2. Fill out a Student Report Form outlining the student's progress. Return it to the child's teacher.

Follow-up

- Provide the child you tutored with any additional learning material that he or she might enjoy.
- Send the child you tutored a "friendship card" expressing your pleasure in having had the chance to meet and work with him or her.
- With your small group, hold a party at school for the children that you tutored.